Introduction

Which common children's game was once an Olympic sport? Why did pirates actually wear eyepatches? And why is airplane food bland?

Dive into a fascinating world of mind-boggling, surprising, and life-changing facts about science and history with answers to questions you've always wondered about, and plenty you've never even thought to consider. "Awesome Facts That Will Make You Look Super Smart" is a sensational resource for curious minds who can never get enough of interesting trivia.

Kids and adults alike will become instant trivia champs about science and history!
The perfect gift for yourself or for your fact-loving friend or child, "Awesome Facts That Will Make You Look Super Smart" is the ultimate icebreaker and conversation starter. Get it now and start your adventure of discovery today!

But wait, there's more! Seize the fun and test yourself and others with 50 trivia questions!

LAUGHING
IS CONTAGIOUS, FOR REAL.

THE "TANGANYIKA LAUGHTER EPIDEMIC" INFECTED OVER A THOUSAND PEOPLE IN 1962

IS LAUGHING REALLY CONTAGIOUS?

In 1962, a mysterious laughing epidemic occurred in Tanganyika, which is now part of Tanzania. The event is commonly known as the "Tanganyika laughter epidemic." The outbreak started at a boarding school in the village of Kashasha when three girls began laughing uncontrollably for no apparent reason. The laughter quickly spread to other students, and the epidemic continued to escalate, infecting over a thousand people, including students from other schools in the region. The laughter episodes were often accompanied by other symptoms, such as crying, fainting, and respiratory problems. The epidemic became so severe that many schools in the area had to be temporarily closed to contain the spread of the laughter. The exact cause of the laughter epidemic remains uncertain, and it has been the subject of much speculation and study by researchers. Various factors, including mass hysteria, stress, and social factors, have been suggested as possible contributors to the outbreak. However, the Tanganyika laughter epidemic remains a fascinating and unusual event in the annals of medical and sociological history

No number from 1 to 999 includes the letter "a" in its word form

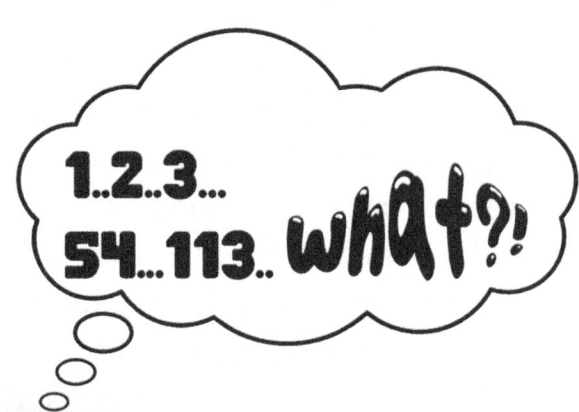

NOMITO CREATIVE STUDIO

AWESOME FACTS

That Will Make You Look Super Smart

Science & History

Producer & International Distributor
Nomito Creative Studio

Interesting Fun Facts For Trivia Lovers:
Awesome Facts That Will Make You Look Super Smart: Science & History

Nomito Creative Studio

Copyright © 2023 Nomito Creative Studio

All rights reserved; No parts of this book may be reproduced or transmitted in any form or by any means, electronic or mechanical, including photocopying, recording, taping, or by any information retrieval system, without the permission, in writing, of the author.

Contact: Tominomiltd@gmail.com
ISBN 9798870071008

Is there a reason why there is no "a" between 1 and 999?

When you consider numbers from 1 to 999 and represent them in their word form, you'll notice an interesting linguistic quirk: none of them contain the letter "a." This linguistic oddity makes for a fun observation about the English language and the patterns that emerge when numbers are written out. While it might seem surprising at first, it's a playful reminder of the intricacies of language and the many ways in which words can be composed. So, whether you're discussing math or linguistics, this fact adds a touch of uniqueness to the world of numbers!

THE MOST COMMON PASSWORD IS: "123456."

What's your safe word? "WORD?"

"123456" has consistently ranked as one of the most common and unfortunately insecure passwords used by people across various online platforms. This password is extremely easy to guess and offers minimal security, which makes it a prime target for hackers and cyber-attacks. It's always recommended to use strong and unique passwords to protect personal accounts and sensitive information online. The top five most common passwords, which unfortunately are not secure choices, include:

123456
password
123456789
12345678
12345

Baby Apple is

ONE

SUPERMARKET APPLES CAN BE A YEAR OLD

IS IT POSSIBLE TO BUY A YEAR-OLD APPLE AT THE SUPERMARKET?

Apples are often harvested during their peak season, which varies depending on the variety and location, but it can range from late summer to early fall. To ensure a year-round supply of apples, they are typically stored in controlled environments such as cold storage facilities. These facilities regulate temperature, humidity, and gas levels to slow down the ripening process and extend the shelf life of the apples. When apples are properly stored in these conditions, they can remain fresh and retain their quality for several months. This allows consumers to enjoy apples throughout the year, even when they are not in season locally. So, it's not uncommon to find apples in supermarkets that were harvested many months before they are purchased.

Pubs in Turkey used to employ special porters, who carried customers who were too drunk to walk on their backs

What do "hamals" us about Turkish hospitality traditions?

In the not-so-distant past, pubs in Turkey had a unique and practical solution for customers who had indulged a bit too much in their libations. Specialized porters, affectionately known as "hamals" or sırtçılar, were employed to carry inebriated patrons on their backs or shoulders when they could no longer walk. This peculiar service, while seemingly humorous, had a practical purpose: ensuring the safety and welfare of individuals who had overindulged. It also reflected a different era in the social and cultural landscape of Turkey, where the responsibilities of hospitality extended beyond just serving drinks. However, as times have changed and alcohol-related regulations and attitudes have evolved, this once-common practice has largely faded into the annals of history, a reminder of the colorful and unique traditions that can be found in different corners of the world.

There is a plane ticket that can be used to go around the world

There are plane tickets known as "round-the-world" or "RTW" tickets that can be used to travel around the world. The ticket itself cannot be bought from one airline but from an airline alliance (there are three major alliances in the world – Star Alliance, Sky Team, One World) and all flights are made by the airlines belonging to the alliance. To embark on a round-the-world journey, pick a starting point, decide if you'll go east or west, then select your destinations in advance. Travel in one continuous direction until you complete a loop back to your initial spot, all within the ticket's validity period, typically one year (though shorter options may exist, like 80 days). Plan wisely, and explore the globe at your pace.

IN A DAY, A PERSON CAN PRODUCE ENOUGH SALIVA TO FILL A 32 OZ. BOTTLE

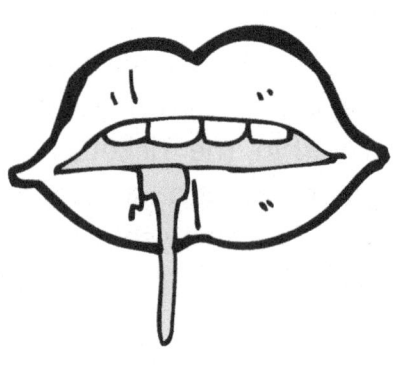

WHY DOES A PERSON PRODUCE ENOUGH SALIVA IN A DAY TO FILL A 32 FL. OZ. BOTTLE?

Due to the crucial role of saliva in maintaining oral health and facilitating the process of digestion. Saliva is produced by three pairs of major salivary glands (parotid, submandibular, and sublingual) along with numerous minor glands in the mouth. On average, individuals produce about 0.5 to 1.5 liters of saliva daily, depending on factors such as age, overall health, and diet. Saliva serves essential functions, including moistening food to aid in swallowing, initiating the digestion of starches through enzymes like amylase, and neutralizing acids to protect tooth enamel. Moreover, saliva helps maintain oral hygiene by washing away debris and harmful bacteria, promoting a balanced and healthy environment in the mouth. This abundant production of saliva is essential for maintaining optimal oral health and supporting efficient digestion throughout the day.

With two fingers covering your nose, you can't hum any song.

Yes, you can leave the book and try it now.

We know you were skeptical, but now that you have the proof, learn why it's not possible.

If you cover your nose with two fingers while attempting to hum a song, you will likely find it challenging or impossible to produce the humming sound. When you hum, the air you exhale from your lungs passes through your vocal cords and resonates in your nasal cavity, creating the humming sound. Covering your nose with your fingers restricts the airflow through your nasal passage, preventing the air from resonating and significantly affecting the humming sound. As a result, the humming may sound muffled, or you may not be able to produce any humming sound at all. Try it out for yourself and see how covering your nose impacts your ability to hum a song!

Around 100 muscles are activated when speaking

Which muscles are activated when speaking, and why so many?

Speaking is a remarkably intricate process that engages some 100 muscles in the human body. When we communicate, these muscles work harmoniously to produce the sounds and words we use to convey our thoughts, emotions, and ideas. The process begins with the diaphragm and intercostal muscles, which control the expansion and contraction of the lungs, allowing us to breathe in and out. The articulation of speech sounds is another crucial aspect, involving the precise coordination of various muscles in the tongue, lips, jaw, and soft palate. These muscles shape the flow of air from the vocal cords into distinct speech sounds and combine them to form words and sentences. Additionally, facial muscles play a role in non-verbal communication, such as expressing emotions and emphasizing certain aspects of speech. From the intricate coordination of the muscles involved in breathing, voice production, and articulation, speaking is an extraordinary feat that showcases the complexity and versatility of the human body.

YOUR BODY CONTAINS ABOUT

100,000

MILES OF BLOOD VESSELS

HOW LONG IS OUR BODY'S INTRICATE NETWORK OF BLOOD VESSELS, AND WHAT'S ITS ASTONISHING COMPARISON?

Our bodies host an amazing spectacle – an intricate web of blood vessels that spans around 100,000 miles (that's about 160,934 kilometers). Yep, you heard right – it's like having a secret highway system inside! These arteries, veins, and capillaries work like busy messengers, shuttling oxygen, nutrients, and all sorts of essential goodies to our cells, while giving waste products the boot. But hold on to your hat – that 160,934 kilometers isn't just any number. It's like circling the Earth's equator four times or even shooting off to the Moon! So, while we're not launching into space, our body's inner highway system is a journey all its own!

YAWNING
EXPLAINED:

The average yawn lasts six seconds. Humans also yawn on average 20 times per day, so in total, that's 120 seconds or two whole minutes you spend yawning each day. Yawning is contagious, so even reading this, and thinking about yawning, might make you yawn. (Bet you a zillion bucks you just yawned. Are we right?)

WHAT'S GOING ON WITH ALL THIS YAWNING?

Yawning, the timeless mystery that has kept scientists guessing, is a phenomenon with multiple captivating theories. From regulating oxygen levels by taking in a deep breath during a yawn to potentially cooling the brain as an influx of air lowers its temperature, yawning has intrigued experts for its multifaceted nature. Its role in boosting alertness, possibly signaling group rest through its contagiousness, and even serving as a stress-relief mechanism in response to anxiety have all been proposed. Despite these intriguing ideas, the true essence of yawning remains an ongoing puzzle, eagerly studied to unlock its secrets.

You can't lick your elbow

Okay, so there are a few people who might be able to lick their own elbows, but it's very rare, and you'd need to have short arms.

So why not give it a go and see if you can do it?

Sweat doesn't smell bad

Does people's sweat make them stink?

While sweat itself is odorless, the unpleasant smell often associated with sweat is actually caused by bacteria on the skin breaking down the components of sweat. When sweat interacts with these bacteria, it can produce a distinct and sometimes unpleasant odor. This is particularly true for sweat produced in areas with a high concentration of apocrine sweat glands, such as the armpits and groin, which release a different type of sweat that is richer in proteins and fatty acids, providing more fuel for bacterial growth and odor.

Like fingerprints, everyone's tongue print is different

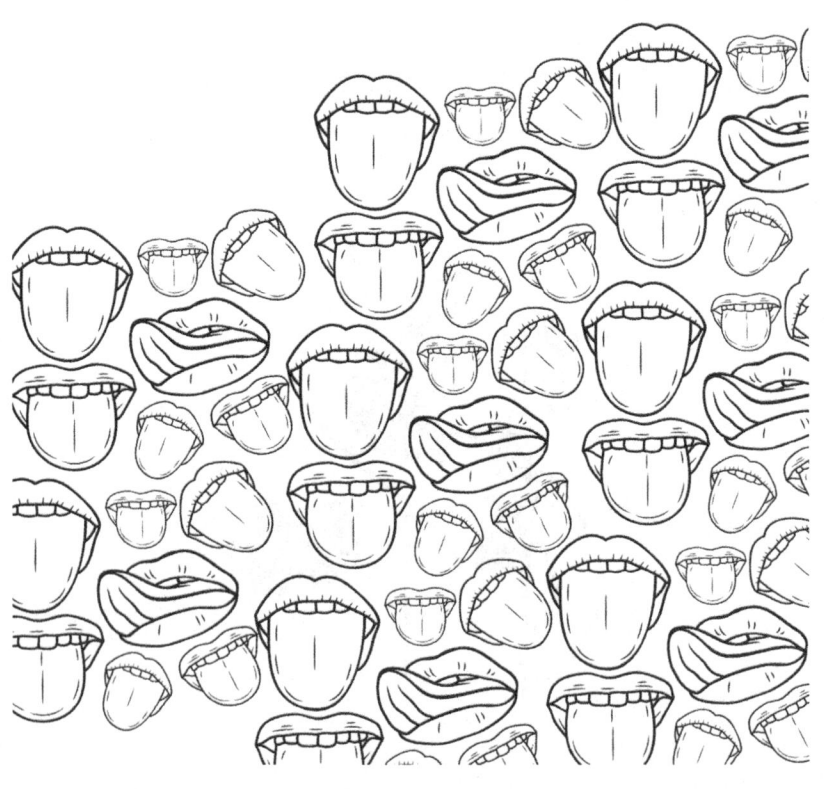

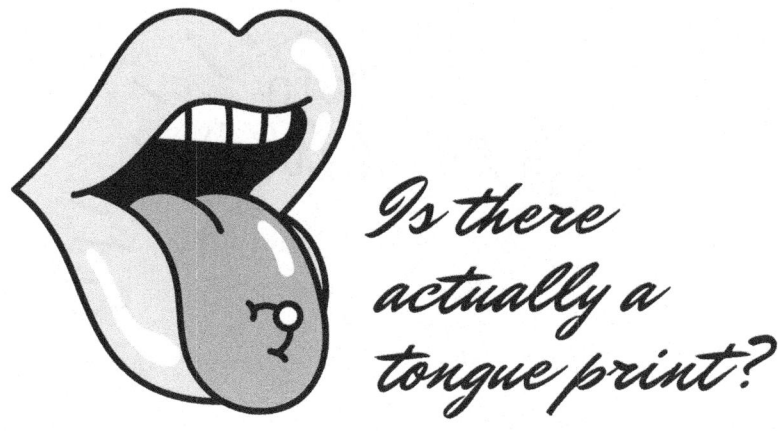

Is there actually a tongue print?

The unique patterns and features on a person's tongue can be used for identification purposes, just like fingerprints. However, tongue prints are not as commonly used or as reliable for identification as fingerprints, which are more detailed and consistent. While tongue prints can vary from person to person, they have not been widely adopted for forensic or identification purposes due to their less distinct and consistent nature compared to fingerprints. Fingerprints remain the primary biometric identifier used in law enforcement and various security applications.

Household dust is primarily composed of dead skin cells

Why is our home dust so full of dead skin cells?

Dust in homes consists of various particles and debris, including dead skin cells shed by humans and pets, Humans naturally shed millions of skin cells every day as part of the body's normal process of renewal and regeneration. These dead skin cells are released from the outermost layer of the skin (the epidermis) and are replaced by new cells from below. Additionally, household dust can contain other materials such as pollen, lint, dust mites, pet dander, and microscopic particles from various sources. Dead skin cells are continually being shed from our bodies and can accumulate on surfaces, contributing to the formation of household dust. Regular cleaning and dusting help reduce the buildup of dust and allergens in indoor environments.

What Is eigengrau, and how does it illustrate human perception in absolute darkness?

"Eigengrau" is a real color known as "intrinsic gray" or "eigenlicht." It's the dark gray hue that the human eye perceives in absolute darkness or when eyes are closed. This phenomenon arises from the random activity of photoreceptor cells in the retina when no external light is present. While some might perceive it as pure black, it's technically a very dark shade of gray. Eigengrau represents the absence of visible light and serves as an intriguing concept in the field of human perception and vision, illustrating that even in the absence of external stimuli, our eyes continue to send signals to our brain, creating a sensation of this subtle grayish hue.

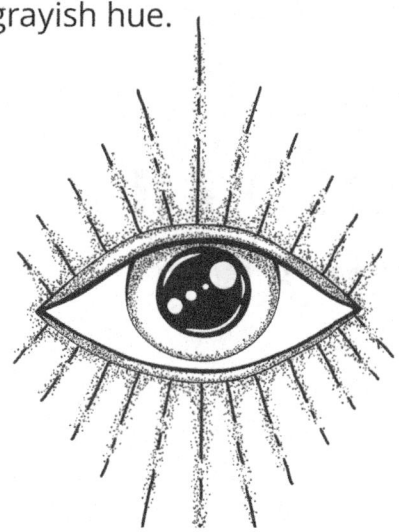

RAIN OF FISH

IS AN ANNUAL WEATHER EVENT IN WHICH HUNDREDS OF FISH RAIN FROM THE SKY ONTO THE HONDURAN CITY OF YORO

WHY DO FISH RAIN FROM THE SKY IN YORO, HONDURAS?

In the Honduran city of Yoro, a remarkable annual event known as the "Rain of Fish" captivates both residents and curious visitors alike. During heavy rainstorms, hundreds of small fish, locally known as "matechines," inexplicably fall from the sky. This captivating natural phenomenon has been a long-standing tradition in Yoro and continues to be a source of wonder and intrigue. Scientists have ventured various theories to explain this occurrence, including the possibility of waterspouts lifting the fish from nearby bodies of water and depositing them in the rain. Regardless of the cause, the "Rain of Fish" remains a testament to the mysteries of nature and the enduring wonder it can inspire in the hearts of those who witness it.

Ketchup
was used as medicine during the 19th century

(And it still is for my father's food...)

Ketchup as a medicine?

In the 19th century, ketchup was indeed used for medicinal purposes. The early origins of ketchup can be traced back to Asia, where it was initially a sauce made from various ingredients like fermented fish or soybeans. These early versions of ketchup were believed to have health benefits and were used for medicinal purposes. When ketchup made its way to Europe and America, its composition changed to include tomatoes, vinegar, and various spices. During the 19th century, some believed that the acidic and spiced nature of ketchup could aid in digestion and improve overall health. It was often promoted as a remedy for digestive issues, such as indigestion and diarrhea. As time went on, ketchup's association with medicine diminished, and it transformed into the popular condiment we know today. While modern ketchup is no longer used as medicine, it remains a beloved and versatile sauce enjoyed with a wide range of foods worldwide.

The Train was invented before the bicycle

From steam to spokes:
The train's preceding path to Invention before the bicycle.

Believe it or not, the train chugged onto the scene before the bicycle even had a chance to pedal in! Back in 1804, the "Puffing Devil," a steam-powered locomotive, stole the show with its transportation magic. But hold your horses (or should we say bikes?) – the pedal-powered wonder we now call a bicycle didn't start cruising until the 19th century. Karl Drais got the ball rolling in 1817 with his "dandy horse," and it wasn't until the 1860s that the modern bike's pedals and chain drive brought a whole new spin to the game. Who knew those train tracks got laid down before the pedaling frenzy began?

ANCIENT EGYPTIANS USED DEAD MICE TO EASE TOOTHACHES

WHY DID ANCIENT EGYPTIANS USE DEAD MICE TO EASE TOOTHACHES?

In ancient Egypt, they believed that the application of a dead mouse to a painful tooth could help alleviate the pain. This practice is recorded in some historical accounts and is an example of the early folk remedies used by different cultures to address various ailments, including toothaches. It's important to note that medical practices and knowledge have evolved significantly since ancient times and modern dentistry provides more effective and safe treatments for dental issues.

PIRATES WORE EYE PATCHES TO ADJUST TO THE LIGHT AND DARKNESS ABOVE AND BELOW DECK DURING RAIDS

EYERRRR PATCH

Pirates commonly wore eye patches not for just an iconic look but for practical purposes. It helped them adjust to differing light conditions above and below deck during their raids. By keeping one eye accustomed to darkness with the eye patch, they preserved their night vision below deck. When they emerged into the bright sunlight, they could switch the eye patch to the other eye, allowing them to quickly adapt to the increased light levels. This practice helped them navigate the varying light conditions on their ships effectively and avoid temporary blindness. Additionally, eye patches could also be used to conceal injuries, adding to the mystery and intrigue associated with pirates.

 The King of Hearts is the only king in a deck of cards without a mustache

♡ Meet the best-shaven king:

There are a few intriguing assumptions about why the King of Hearts stands alone as the sole king without a mustache. One suggests that diamonds, clubs, and spades are often associated respectively with wealth, war, and death – definitely some heavy stuff. In contrast, the heart symbolizes purity, openness, and genuine emotion. So, maybe the King of Hearts went for the clean-shaven look to match the unadorned authenticity of the heart. On the historical front, here's another guess: When playing cards were first crafted back in the 16th century, they were a masterpiece of woodblock printing. However, as time passed and unskilled artisans tinkered with the designs, things got a bit wonky. Among the changes, the King of Hearts saw his axe become a sword, and coincidentally, his mustache disappeared. Maybe it was a case of artistic evolution gone a bit haywire. So, which version seems to hit the jackpot? The next time you're enjoying a card game, take a moment to ponder these playful possibilities behind the enigmatic clean-shaven king.

Tug-of-War was once an Olympic sport

Why was Tug-of-War an Olympic sport and why did it disappear?

Tug-of-War, a classic team competition that involves two groups vying to pull a rope in opposing directions, holds a unique place in Olympic history. It was a legitimate Olympic sport from 1900 through 1920, featuring prominently in the early editions of the modern Olympic Games. Teams of athletes showcased their strength, coordination, and teamwork as they battled to drag their opponents over a specified distance or marker. However, despite its popularity during that era, tug-of-war was eventually removed from the Olympic program after the 1920 Antwerp Olympics. The reasons for its departure remain a matter of historical debate, but the sport has not made a return to the modern Olympic Games since then, making it a fascinating relic of Olympic history.

Before alarm clocks, there were "knocker-uppers."

How did "Knocker-Uppers" serve as human alarm clocks before modern technology?

Before the widespread availability of alarm clocks, especially in the 19th and early 20th centuries, there were individuals known as "knocker-uppers" or "human alarm clocks" who performed the task of waking people up in the morning. These knocker-uppers were often hired or employed to go around neighborhoods and use long sticks or poles to tap on windows or doors to wake their clients at the requested time. It was a form of personalized wake-up service that helped people get to work or appointments on time in the absence of alarm clocks. This practice was more common in urban areas and industrial towns during the period when alarm clocks were not as affordable or widespread.

In 18th century England, pineapples were a symbol of status

Why were pineapples a symbol of wealth?

In 18th-century England, pineapples were considered a symbol of status and wealth. Pineapples were rare and exotic fruits at the time, and their high cost and limited availability made them a luxury item. As a result, people with the means to do so would often display pineapples at social gatherings, and even rent them for special occasions to showcase their affluence. Pineapples became a symbol of hospitality and prestige, and they were prominently featured in architecture, art, and interior design as a way to demonstrate one's social standing. This trend eventually led to the creation of decorative elements like pineapple-shaped finials on gateposts and bedposts, which can still be seen in some historic buildings today.

That tiny pocket in jeans was designed to store pocket watches.

The Origin of the Tiny Pocket:

The jeans' small pocket, sometimes referred to as a "watch pocket," dates back to the 19th century when pocket watches were more common and needed a secure and easily accessible place for storage. In the days when pocket watches were a common accessory, jeans manufacturers included this small pocket as a practical feature to accommodate the needs of their customers. While pocket watches are no longer as prevalent, the tiny pocket has remained a design element in many jeans as a nod to the history of denim and fashion.

A mysterious dance epidemic caused 400 people to dance uncontrollably, resulting in numerous deaths

The unexplained "Dance Epidemic of 1518" – a mysterious and deadly outbreak in Strasbourg's history?

The "Dance Epidemic of 1518" remains a captivating historical mystery that unfolded in the heart of Strasbourg, Alsace, a region within the Holy Roman Empire. In the sweltering summer of 1518, something inexplicable gripped the population, as around 400 individuals took to the streets and were consumed by an uncontrollable urge to dance. This bizarre phenomenon endured for weeks on end, with dancers displaying an eerie combination of ecstasy and exhaustion. Tragically, the relentless dancing led to numerous fatalities, with some succumbing to heart attacks, strokes, hunger, or sheer physical exhaustion. The roots of this peculiar episode remain elusive, with theories suggesting a complex interplay of psychological stress, societal influences, and perhaps even the effects of ergot poisoning from contaminated grains. The Dancing Plague of 1518 remains a testament to the enigmatic facets of human behavior, leaving an indelible mark on the annals of history.

The first year AD is the year 1. An interesting fact is that the previous year isn't 0, but the year 1 BC

How does this quirk calendar fact shape our understanding of historical dates?

The fact that the first year AD is designated as the year 1 and that the year immediately before it is known as 1 BC is a quirk of our modern Gregorian calendar system. This unusual numbering system arises from the historical context in which the calendar was developed. At the time, the concept of zero as a numerical placeholder was not widely used or understood in the Western world. As a result, the creators of the calendar opted to transition directly from 1 BC to 1 AD, without an intervening year 0. While this numbering convention may seem counterintuitive, it has become deeply ingrained in our calendar system, shaping how we perceive historical dates and timelines. Despite its idiosyncrasies, the Gregorian calendar remains the most widely accepted and used calendar system today, reflecting the intricate interplay between history, mathematics, and cultural norms.

An espresso maker was sent into space in 2015

But first, coffee:

The espresso machine, called the "ISSpresso," was delivered to the International Space Station (ISS) aboard a SpaceX Dragon spacecraft in April 2015. It was a collaboration between the Italian Space Agency, Argotec (an engineering company), and the coffee brand Lavazza. The ISSpresso machine allowed astronauts aboard the ISS to enjoy freshly brewed espresso coffee while in orbit, marking a significant improvement in their quality of life and dietary options during their missions.

Forget your Big Macs - McDonald's originally sold hot dogs, not burgers

HotDognalds?

The first McDonald's restaurant, opened by Richard and Maurice McDonald in 1940 in San Bernardino, California, primarily featured a menu centered around hot dogs and other items such as milkshakes, coffee, and pie. It was only later, when Ray Kroc joined the company in 1954 and began franchising the brand, that the menu was revamped to focus on hamburgers, cheeseburgers, and the iconic Big Mac. The shift to a burger-centric menu marked a significant turning point in the history of McDonald's, and it became one of the world's most recognizable fast-food chains.

Originally, Ben & Jerry's was going to be a bagel company

Could it be everything delight?

The company was founded by Ben Cohen and Jerry Greenfield in 1978 in Burlington, Vermont. They initially set out to start a bagel business but found the cost of bagel-making equipment to be too high. As a result, they decided to pursue making ice cream instead, which required less initial investment in equipment. Their decision to make ice cream led to the creation of the unique and innovative ice cream flavors for which Ben & Jerry's is now famous. The company's socially conscious approach to business and its commitment to using high-quality ingredients have also been key factors in its success.

SALT USED TO BE A CURRENCY

HOW DID SALT SERVE AS CURRENCY IN ANCIENT SOCIETIES?

Salt was used as a form of currency in various ancient societies due to its essential role in preserving and flavoring food, as well as its other industrial and medicinal uses. Notably, the Roman Empire paid its soldiers in salt, leading to the term "salary." Salt blocks or bars were also used for trade in certain African cultures. This historical practice underscores the immense value placed on salt in different civilizations, shaping its role as a currency alongside its culinary importance.

The amazing NAKAM team

Nakam, which loosely translated means "Avengers" in Hebrew, was a group of Jewish survivors of the Holocaust who, fueled by a deep desire for justice and retribution, embarked on a mission to hold Nazi war criminals accountable for their heinous actions. Formed in the immediate aftermath of World War II, Nakam sought to avenge the suffering and loss endured by Jewish communities during the Holocaust. Their most infamous plan, "Operation Kutschera," aimed to poison the water supply of a POW camp for German SS officers. While this operation was ultimately abandoned, Nakam's existence serves as a testament to the profound trauma of the Holocaust and the determination of survivors to seek a form of justice in the tumultuous aftermath of the war, even though their efforts remained largely unfulfilled.

Google's founders were willing to sell **Google** for under $1million in 1999

1,000,000

A missed opportunity that shaped tech history

In 1999, Larry Page and Sergey Brin, the two graduate students from Stanford University who had founded Google in a garage, were actively seeking investors to support their growing search engine project. At the time, Excite was one of the leading internet companies and search engines, and Google was struggling financially. Page and Brin offered to sell Google to Excite for just under $1 million, with the condition that they would maintain control of the search engine's technology. Excite, led by CEO George Bell, declined the offer. The decision was influenced by a variety of factors, including concerns about Google's unproven revenue model. This turned out to be one of the most significant missed opportunities in tech history. Google went on to revolutionize internet search, online advertising, and various other digital services, eventually becoming one of the world's most valuable and influential technology companies. In contrast, Excite's fortunes declined over the years, highlighting the incredible divergence in the paths of these two companies following that pivotal decision.

PLEASE KEEP YOUR SEATBELT FASTENED AT ALL TIMES...

The flight route connects the Orkney Islands of Westray and Papa Westray, both located in the northern part of Scotland. The flight distance between these two islands is exceptionally short, with a Guinness World Record-setting flight time of just a couple of minutes on certain occasions. The distance between the airports is approximately 1.7 miles (2.7 kilometers). The flight is primarily used by local residents and is known for its brevity, making it a unique and fascinating experience for travelers.

MOMMMY I'm bored!!!

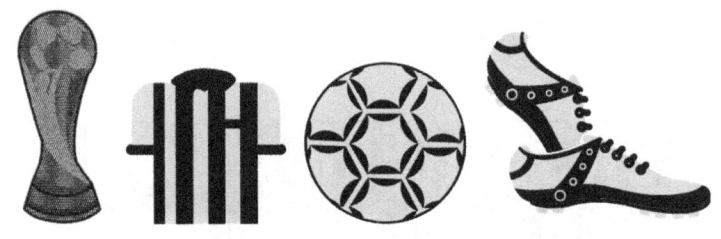

IN THE FIFA WORLD CUP QUALIFYING MATCH ON APRIL 11, 2001, AUSTRALIA DEFEATED AMERICAN SAMOA 31-0

How did Australia achieve this astounding victory?

April 11, 2001, marked a remarkable and, in some ways, unbelievable chapter in the annals of international football. On that fateful day, the Australian national football team faced off against the American Samoa team in a FIFA World Cup qualification match. What ensued was a goal-scoring spectacle of epic proportions, as Australia trounced their opponents with a jaw-dropping scoreline of 31-0. This astonishing victory not only showcased Australia's football prowess but also raised eyebrows worldwide. With each goal, the scoreboard seemed to defy logic, and the match went down in history as one of the most lopsided victories ever recorded in the beautiful game. While it was a memorable day for Australian football, it also served as a poignant reminder of the stark disparities that can exist in the world of sports.

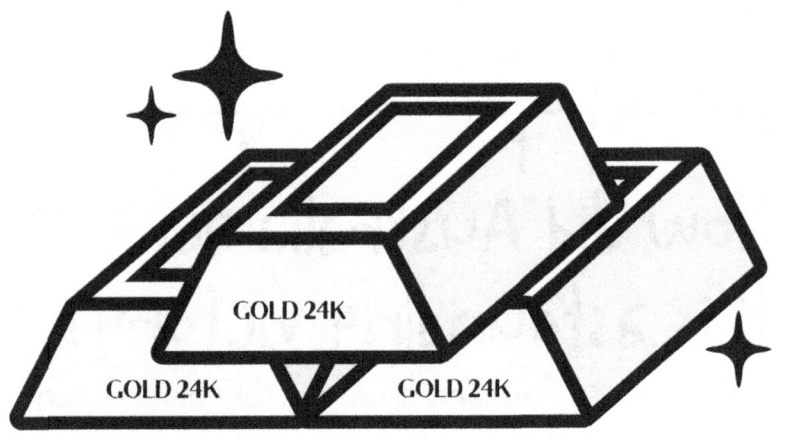

There are very few chemicals found in the earth that can remain undamaged, even after being buried under the ground

What makes gold so durable?

Gold retains its bright shine even after being buried underground because it is highly resistant to corrosion and chemical reactions. This precious metal is considered a noble metal because it does not readily react with most of the chemicals found in the Earth's crust. It remains unresponsive to oxygen, water, and many acids, which prevents tarnishing, rusting, or corrosion over time. This exceptional chemical stability has made gold a valued resource for centuries, prized for its enduring beauty and utility in various applications, from crafting jewelry to minting coins.

Honey never spoils

Now that's an expiry date I can live with

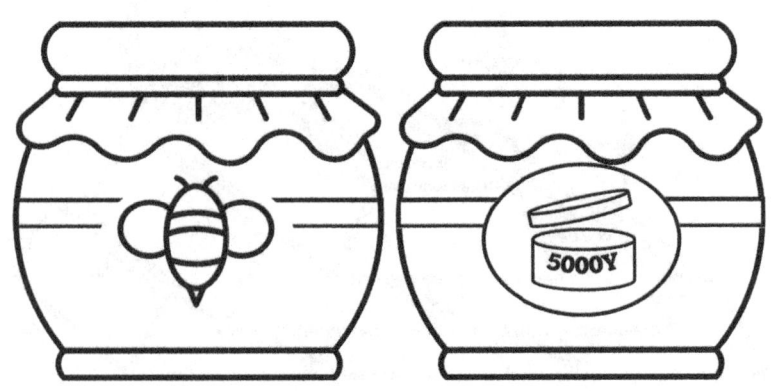

Can you eat honey even 5,000 years after production?

One of the oldest pots of honey that has been found and confirmed to still be good is the "world's oldest honey" discovered in Georgia. Archaeologists found clay pots containing honey in a tomb in the country of Georgia that dates back over 5,000 years to the Bronze Age. The honey was analyzed by scientists, and they determined that it was still safe to eat. The well-sealed clay pots and the natural properties of honey, such as its low water content and acidity, contributed to its preservation over such an extended period. It's important to note that the honey found in this archaeological discovery was still edible after being stored for over 5,000 years. However, it's likely that the texture and taste of the honey may have changed over time. While honey has an impressive ability to resist spoilage, its quality can be affected by factors like temperature, moisture, and light exposure. Properly stored honey can retain its best quality for an extended period, but it's always a good idea to check its sensory attributes before consuming it if it has been stored for an exceptionally long time.

IF YOU CRACK AN EGG IN THE DEPTHS OF THE OCEAN, IT WILL REMAIN INTACT

How come an egg remains whole when cracked in the deep?

If you crack an egg in the depths of the ocean, it will remain intact due to the immense pressure that exists at great depths in the ocean.

The pressure in the ocean increases with depth, and at certain depths, it becomes so intense that it can crush objects that are not specifically designed to withstand it. The pressure at the deepest parts of the ocean, such as the Mariana Trench, can be several thousand times greater than atmospheric pressure at sea level.

When an egg is cracked in the deep ocean, the pressure acting on it from all directions prevents the egg from collapsing or breaking apart. This phenomenon is often used as an analogy to explain the concept of pressure in the ocean's depths and the need for specially designed equipment, such as deep-sea submarines and underwater vehicles, to

Botanically speaking, The banana isn't a fruit

Why don't botanists consider banana a fruit?

Botanically speaking, the banana is not classified as a true fruit in the same sense as many other fruits. Instead, it is considered a "false fruit" or a "parthenocarpic berry."

In botanical terms, a fruit is the mature ovary of a flowering plant that contains seeds. However, in the case of bananas, they are typically seedless due to parthenocarpy, a natural process in which the fruit develops without fertilization. This means that the bananas we commonly eat do not contain seeds like traditional fruits.

The banana plant's reproductive structures are more complex than a typical fruit-bearing plant. The seeds are tiny and not fully developed, which makes the banana a unique example of a false fruit.

While bananas may not fit the strict botanical definition of a fruit, they are still widely regarded as fruits in common language and culinary usage due to their sweet taste, soft texture, and the way they are used in various dishes and desserts.

JUPITER IS TWICE AS MASSIVE AS ALL THE OTHER PLANETS COMBINED

LET'S TALK ABOUT JUPITER

Jupiter is indeed more massive than all the other planets in our solar system combined. Its immense size and mass make it a dominant presence in our planetary neighborhood.

Jupiter's mass is approximately 318 times that of Earth, and its sheer size allows it to have a strong gravitational influence on its surroundings. Its mass is so significant that it plays a crucial role in shaping the dynamics of the solar system, particularly in terms of gravitational interactions with other planets and celestial bodies. This fact showcases the extraordinary scale and diversity of celestial bodies within our solar system.

Why did Venus decide to go against the planetary flow and do the "moonwalk" of rotations?

Venus, the second planet from the Sun, stands out in our solar system for its unique rotation. Unlike most planets that rotate counterclockwise, Venus rotates clockwise on its axis. This phenomenon, known as retrograde rotation, makes Venus the only planet to exhibit such a clockwise spin. This distinctive characteristic sets Venus apart in our celestial neighborhood and adds to the fascinating diversity of planetary behavior within our solar system.

When the moon is directly overhead, you will weigh slightly less

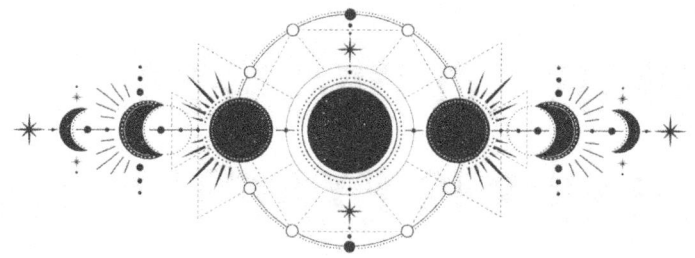

Why are we thinner when the moon is directly over our head?

This phenomenon occurs due to the gravitational interaction between the Earth, the Moon, and your body. When the Moon is directly overhead, it exerts a slightly stronger gravitational force on the side of the Earth facing it. This results in a slightly reduced gravitational force on objects on the Earth's surface, including you. However, the change in weight is extremely small and usually not noticeable in everyday situations. The difference in weight is typically in the order of a few milligrams (thousandths of a gram) and is insignificant for most practical purposes.

MINUS 40 DEGREES CELSIUS IS EXACTLY THE SAME AS MINUS 40 DEGREES FAHRENHEIT

How is this temperature balance possible?

The temperature scales of Celsius and Fahrenheit intersect at -40 degrees, making them equal at this specific temperature point. This is one of the few temperature values where the two scales align. In most other cases, Celsius and Fahrenheit temperatures are different and require conversion to compare.

A DAY ON VENUS IS LONGER THAN ITS YEAR

A DAY IS LONGER THAN A YEAR? MAKE IT MAKE SENSE!

Venus has an extremely slow rotation on its axis, taking approximately 243 Earth days to complete one full rotation. In contrast, Venus' orbital period around the Sun, which defines its year, is about 225 Earth days. This means that a day on Venus, measured by its rotation, is longer than a year on Venus, measured by its orbit around the Sun. It's one of the most unusual aspects of Venus's planetary characteristics. Additionally, Venus' rotation is also retrograde, meaning it rotates in the opposite direction to most planets, including Earth.

WHY DOES THE EIFFEL TOWER GROW TALLER DURING HOT DAYS?

The Eiffel Tower is made of iron, which expands when exposed to heat and contracts when it cools down. This property of metal is known as thermal expansion. On a hot day, the iron structure of the Eiffel Tower can absorb heat from the Sun, causing the metal to expand. As a result, the tower's height can increase by several inches during periods of high temperature. Conversely, during cooler nights, the tower contracts, and its height decreases. The expansion and contraction of the Eiffel Tower due to temperature fluctuations are relatively small and not easily noticeable, but they are a well-documented phenomenon associated with metal structures.

Airplane food isn't very tasty because our sense of smell and taste decrease by 20 to 50 percent during flights

Chicken or beef?

Airplane food has long been the subject of jokes and complaints, and the phenomenon of diminished taste perception during flights sheds light on this culinary mystery. It's a fact that our sense of smell and taste can decline significantly, ranging from 20 to 50 percent, when we're up in the air. This phenomenon is due to a combination of factors, including the dry and low-humidity cabin air, reduced air pressure, and the constant background noise on aircraft. These conditions affect our taste buds and olfactory senses, making it challenging for us to fully savor the flavors of in-flight meals. Airlines are aware of these challenges and often strive to create more robust and flavorful dishes to account for passengers' sensory limitations at high altitudes. So, the unappetizing reputation of airplane food may be, in part, a consequence of the unique conditions of air travel.

THERE MAY BE A PLANET MADE OUT OF DIAMONDS

Can I get a diamond planet please?

These exoplanets, often referred to as "diamond planets," are theoretical and have not been directly observed. The idea is based on scientific models and theories about the composition and conditions on certain exoplanets. In some cases, scientists have theorized that exoplanets with high carbon content and extreme pressure and temperature conditions could potentially host diamond structures in their interiors. However, these are theoretical concepts, and the existence of actual diamond planets remains speculative. The study of exoplanets is a rapidly evolving field, and new discoveries are made regularly. While the idea of diamond planets is intriguing, it's important to note that our understanding of exoplanets is still developing, and further research and observations are needed to confirm the existence of such planets.

HEIGHTENING IN SPACE

Astronauts grow taller in space due to the absence of Earth's gravity compressing their spines. This phenomenon occurs as the intervertebral discs in their spines expand in the microgravity environment. On average, astronauts can temporarily gain between 2 to 5 centimeters (about 0.8 to 2 inches) in height while in space. However, it's essential to understand that this height increase is only temporary, as their spines gradually return to their normal length upon their return to Earth and exposure to gravity. This natural adaptation to the microgravity environment is well-documented in space science.

WHY IS THE MOON DRIFTING AWAY FROM EARTH, AND HOW DOES IT AFFECT OUR PLANET?

The Moon's slow but measurable drift away from Earth, known as lunar recession, occurs at a rate of roughly 4 centimeters (1.6 inches) per year. This phenomenon is attributed to gravitational interactions between the Earth and the Moon, leading to a transfer of angular momentum. As the Moon moves slightly farther from our planet over time, it has implications for both Earth's rotation and the Earth-Moon system. Specifically, this gradual separation contributes to a lengthening of Earth's day, as the Moon's gravitational pull on Earth generates tides, which in turn affect the planet's rotation. While the effects are subtle and take place over millions of years, this ongoing process showcases the dynamic nature of celestial bodies and their interactions in our solar system.

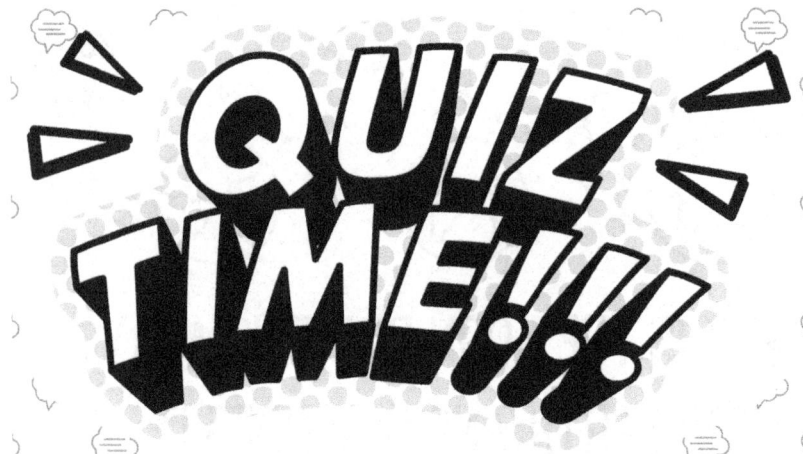

Kudos for finishing the book! But wait, there's more!

Let's see how much of those juicy facts you soaked up.

Bet you're already looking like a smarty-pants, but a quick trivia will seal the deal!

Questions:

Q1: What mysterious event occurred that leading to over a thousand people being infected?
A) The Tanganyika dancing epidemic
B) The Tanganyika crying outbreak
C) The Tanganyika sneezing contagion
D) The Tanganyika laughter epidemic

Q2: Which letter is notably missing in the word forms of numbers from 1 to 999?
A) Letter "b"
B) Letter "a"
C) Letter "c"
D) Letter "d"

Q3: What is consistently ranked as one of the most common and insecure passwords?
A) Your birthday dates
B) q1w2e3r4
C) 123456
D) abcdef

Q4: How old can supermarket apples be?
A) Up to a year old
B) Up to six months old
C) Up to three months old
D) Up to two years old

Q5: What were the employees called in Turkey who carried away drunk customers in pubs?
A) Pub Porters
B) Drunk Escorts
C) hamals
D) Libation Luggers

Q6: How can you travel around the world using a single ticket?
A) By purchasing the ticket directly from any airline.
B) By choosing destinations randomly without any predefined route.
C) By using a "round-the-world" or "RTW" ticket from an airline alliance.
D) By booking separate tickets for each leg of the journey.

Q7: On average, how much saliva can a person produce in a day?
A) 0.5 to 1.5 liters
B) 1 to 2 liters
C) 2 to 3 liters
D) 1.5 to 2.5 liters

Q8: Why is it impossible to hum while covering your nose with two fingers?
A) It causes discomfort and distraction
B) It interferes with the vocal cords
C) It triggers a reflex that inhibits humming
D) It restricts airflow through the nasal passage

Q9: How many muscles are activated when speaking?
A) Around 50 muscles
B) Around 75 muscles
C) Around 100 muscles
D) Around 125 muscles

Q10: How long is the intricate network of blood vessels in the human body?
A) 150,000 miles
B) 100,000 miles
C) 175,000 miles
D) 125,000 miles

Q11: How long, on average, does a yawn last?
A) 6 seconds
B) 4 seconds
C) 10 seconds
D) 8 seconds

Q12: Is it possible for a person to lick their own elbow?
A) Yes, but it's very rare and requires short arms.
B) Absolutely, everyone can easily do it.
C) No, it's physically impossible for anyone.
D) Only if you're a contortionist.

Q13: What causes the unpleasant smell associated with sweat?
A) The sweat itself
B) Perfume or deodorant
C) Fabric worn during sweating
D) Bacteria on the skin breaking down sweat components

Q14: Besides fingerprints, what other prints can be used for identification purposes?
A) Tongue prints
B) Footprints
C) Ear prints
D) Nose prints

Q15: What is the primary component of household dust that accumulates on surfaces?
A) Pollen
B) Pet dander
C) Dead skin cells
D) Dust mites

Q16: What is "eigengrau"?
A) It is a color created by external stimuli in the absence of light.
B) It is a shade of pure black.
C) It is a dark gray hue.
D) It is an optical illusion that occurs when eyes are closed in the dark.

Q17: What mysterious event takes place every year in Yoro, Honduras?
A) The sky turns purple
B) Rain of Fish
C) A smelly breeze
D) Eclipse

Q18: During the 19th century, why was ketchup believed to have medicinal properties?
A) It was thought to cure common colds.
B) Its acidic and spiced nature was believed to aid in digestion.
C) It was used as an antiseptic for wounds.
D) Ketchup was considered a remedy for headaches.

Q19: Which invention came first in history, predating the other?
A) Bicycle
B) Steam-powered locomotive
C) Both were invented simultaneously
D) Electric train

Q20: With what did Ancient Egyptians ease their toothaches?
A) Crushed herbs and spices applied directly to the affected tooth.
B) A concoction of honey and herbs consumed orally for pain relief.
C) Placing dead mice directly on the painful tooth.
D) Chewing on mint leaves to alleviate toothache discomfort.

Q21: Why did pirates commonly wear eye patches?
A) To conceal injuries
B) For an iconic look
C) To enhance night vision below deck
D) To protect their eyes from the sun

Q22: What sets the King of Hearts apart from the other king cards in a deck?
A) He has no mustache
B) He has no weapons
C) He has no crown
D) he has no hair

Q23: In which period was Tug-of-War recognized as an Olympic sport?
A) 1900-1920
B) 1930-1950
C) 1960-1980
D) 1990-2010

Q24: Before the widespread use of alarm clocks, what was the role of "knocker-uppers" in waking people up?
A) They used long sticks or poles to tap on windows or doors.
B) They played music loudly in the streets.
C) They shouted loudly from street corners.
D) They delivered morning newspapers to wake people up.

Q25: What was considered a status symbol in 18th-century England?
A) Tulips
B) Pineapples
C) Sunflowers
D) Watermelons

Q26: What was the original purpose of the tiny pocket in jeans?
A) To store spare change
B) To keep keys secure
C) To hold small snacks
D) To store pocket watches

Q27: What was the cause of the mysterious "Dance Epidemic of 1518" in Strasbourg?
A) Psychological stress
B) Societal influences
C) Ergot poisoning from contaminated grains
D) All of the above

Q28: Why is there no year 0 in the transition from 1 BC to 1 AD in the Gregorian calendar?
A) The concept of zero as a numerical placeholder was not widely used or understood in the Western world at that time.
B) The creators of the calendar wanted to simplify the numbering system.
C) There was a historical event that led to skipping the year 0.
D) The transition from 1 BC to 1 AD was an oversight in the calendar's development.

Q29: In what year was an espresso maker sent into space?
A) 2010
B) 2013
C) 2015
D) 2018

Q30: Which of the following was originally the main item on the menu when the first McDonald's restaurant opened in 1940?
A) Hot dogs
B) Hamburgers
C) Cheeseburgers
D) Big Macs

Q31: What was the original business idea of Ben & Jerry's before they decided to make ice cream?
A) Computers laboratory
B) Bagel company
C) High-quality ingredient business
D) Ice cream equipment manufacturing

Q32: In ancient societies, how did salt serve as a form of currency?
A) Salt was primarily used for construction purposes.
B) Salt was utilized as a religious offering.
C) Salt was exchanged as a means of communication.
D) Salt was valued for its ability to preserve and flavor food.

Q33: What is the name of the group formed by Jewish survivors after World War II?
A) The Nakam Team
B) The Survivors
C) The Holocaust Reconciliation Group
D) The Post-War Avengers Initiative

Q34: Which internet company had the opportunity to acquire Google for just under $1 million in 1999?
A) AOL
B) Yahoo
C) Excite
D) Lycos

Q35: What is the record-setting flight time for the shortest flight in the world?
A) Less than 10 minutes
B) About 15 minutes
C) Approximately 30 minutes
D) More than an hour

Q36: What was the score in the World Cup qualifier match on April 11, 2001 between Australia and American Samoa?
A) 8-7 (Australia won)
B) 10-10
C) 17-12 (Australia won)
D) 31-0 (Australia won)

Q37: What attribute makes gold highly durable even when buried underground? A) Reactivity with oxygen
B) Susceptibility to rust
C) Resistance to corrosion and chemical reactions
D) Tendency to tarnish

Q38: What is the expiration date of honey?
A) 10 years
B) 150 years
C) 380 years
D) Never

Q39: Why does an egg remain intact when cracked in the depths of the ocean?
A) The ocean water is colder at great depths, preventing the egg from breaking.
B) The eggshell undergoes a chemical reaction with the deep-sea environment, making it stronger.
C) The pressure in the ocean at great depths prevents the egg from collapsing.
D) Deep-sea organisms form a protective layer around the cracked egg, preserving its structure.

Q40: What makes botanists consider bananas as "false fruits"?
A) Bananas undergo seedless development through parthenocarpy.
B) Bananas lack the typical characteristics of true fruits.
C) Bananas are classified as nuts in botanical terms.
D) Bananas don't have a mature ovary, disqualifying them as true fruits.

Q41: Which statement accurately describes Jupiter's mass in comparison to all the other planets in our solar system?
A) Jupiter is twice as massive as all the other planets combined.
B) Jupiter is equal in mass to all the other planets combined.
C) Jupiter is half as massive as all the other planets combined.
D) Jupiter is three times less massive than all the other planets combined.

Q42: Which planet in our solar system rotates clockwise on its axis?
A) Venus
B) Earth
C) Mars
D) Jupiter

Q43: What happens when the moon is directly above our heads?
A) Nothing
B) You are getting taller
C) You lose some weight
D) You will gain weight

Q44: At what temperature do Celsius and Fahrenheit scales intersect?
A) -40 degrees
B) 0 degrees
C) 100 degrees
D) -100 degrees

Q45: Which of the following statements about Venus is true?
A) A day on Venus is longer than its year.
B) Venus rotates in the same direction as most planets.
C) Venus' orbital period around the Sun is shorter than Earth's.
D) Venus completes one full rotation on its axis in approximately 100 Earth days.

Q46: Why can the Eiffel Tower grow taller on hot days?
A) The tower absorbs heat from the Sun, causing the metal to contract.
B) The Eiffel Tower is made of wood, which expands in response to high temperatures.
C) Thermal expansion, a property of the iron used in the tower, causes it to grow taller.
D) The tower is equipped with hydraulic mechanisms that increase its height in hot weather.

Q47: Why is airplane food often considered less tasty?
A) High altitudes cause our taste buds to malfunction.
B) Cabin air on airplanes is too humid for proper flavor perception.
C) Airplane food is intentionally bland to accommodate diverse preferences.
D) Our sense of smell and taste decreases by 20 to 50 percent during flights.

Q48: Is there a confirmed existence of a planet made out of diamonds?
A) Yes, several diamond planets have been observed.
B) No, the idea of diamond planets is purely theoretical.
C) Maybe, scientists are still debating the possibility.
D) Occasionally, diamond structures have been found on certain exoplanets.

Q49: What happens to astronauts' height in space?
A) They shrink due to microgravity.
B) They remain the same height.
C) They grow taller temporarily.
D) They permanently gain height.

Q50: Why does the Moon move away from Earth?
A) Solar winds pushing the Moon
B) Earth's magnetic field repelling the Moon
C) Gravitational interactions causing lunar recession
D) Moon's self-propulsion mechanism

Answers:

1. D	16. C	31. B	46. C
2. B	17. B	32. D	47. D
3. C	18. B	33. A	48. B
4. A	19. B	34. C	49. C
5. C	20. C	35. A	50. C
6. C	21. C	36. D	
7. A	22. A	37. C	
8. D	23. A	38. D	
9. C	24. A	39. C	
10. B	25. B	40. A	
11. A	26. D	41. B	
12. A	27. D	42. A	
13. D	28. A	43. C	
14. A	29. C	44. A	
15. C	30. A	45. A	

Follow Us ✚

The fun doesn't have to end here! Join our social media party for daily doses of awesome facts and mind-blowing trivia.

Our fact wizards keep the updates rolling in, so you'll never run out of fresh knowledge to share with your buds or test yourself. Plus, be sure to keep an eye out for the hottest deals on your next book purchase with our seriously great coupons.

Check out "Nomito Knowledge" on all platforms and join the awesome facts community!

Made in the USA
Las Vegas, NV
08 April 2024

88389376R00066